Intercessor Waring For The Will of God
Copyright 2019 Iris Leon

Materials found in this workbook where excerpt by:

Understanding Spiritual Authority by Lifestream Teaching Ministries
Decree of Justic in Relationships by Ryan LeStrange
Prophetic Words: Jamie Rohrbaugh
Dr. Judy Fornara(Spiritual Life Ministries)
Authority to Thread by Rebecca Greenwood

Contact information:

Email: mentorshifts@gmail.com
Web: remnantscribe.live

Justice

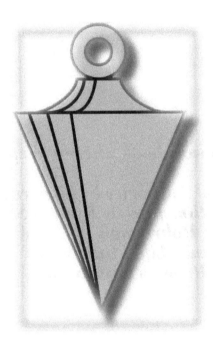

It is a joy for the just to do justice, But destruction will come to the workers of iniquity. Proverbs 21:15

Prophetic Meaning

Number One—Beginning
Number Two—Divide or Judge
Number Three—Conform
Number Four—Rule or Reign
Number Five—Serve
Number Six—Image
Number Seven—Complete
Number Eight—Put Off - New Beginning
Number Nine—Fruit, Harvest or Gifts
Number Ten—Weighed in the Balances
Number Eleven—Last or End

Thirty (three times ten) means "acceptably conformed," or if one is conformed to this world, "unacceptably conformed," but "conformed," nonetheless
Forty means "acceptable" or "unacceptable rule," or rule that has been determined to be good or evil.

Fifty usually relates to ministry
Sixty is the measure of our image
Seventy means complete

Prophetic Meanings of Colors

Colors can be used prophetically in flags, banners, clothing, wall colors ext.. When you are using a color you are basically prophesying these properties.. Like when you use blue flags you are saying "welcome Holy Spirit" ext.. a combination of colors can be used for different reasons..

Black: strength   Blue: water - river of God, cleansing life-giving flow of the Holy Spirit, the Word ruler ship, unlimited potential, priesthood (Esther 8:15), tabernacle (Exodus 25:4)   Light Blue: Holy Spirit, the heavens, Gods throne (Ezekiel 10:1)

Brown: humanity, humility, good soil

Gold: glory, divinity, refinement, purification (Jeremiah 9:7) (Zechariah 13:9), (Job 23:10) Spirit, priesthood, tabernacle (Exodus 25:3) Green: prosperity, health, growth, prophetic, wealth Green Emerald: royalty (Ezekiel 28:13), eternity, faith, Heaven (Revelation 21:19)

Light Green: new life, new beginnings

Orange: fire, proven in fire, power, harvest

Pink: love, compassion, the heart of God

Purple: royalty, kingship, majesty, sonship, priesthood, tabernacle (Exodus 25:4) Red: blood of Jesus, atonement, grace

Silver: redemption, wisdom, the soul (Ecclesiastes 12:6), purification (Zechariah 13:9), priesthood, tabernacle (Exodus 25:3)

White: purity, holiness, righteousness, triumph, (Revelation 7:9) (Revelation 19:14) the bride of Christ

Understanding Spiritual Authority

Before we talk about moving into ministry, lets recap some basic principles that we have learned in these studies.

➤ Lawlessness is the spirit of doing our own thing.

➤ Rebellion is an attitude.

➤ Commandments are specific instructions given by someone in authority.

➤ Obedience to commandments is expected.

➤ Obedience is not automatic; it is learned behavior.

➤ It is an individual choice to resist or submit.

➤ Resist means to "stand against" and submit means to "stand under".

We should keep all of these principles is mind as we move into our study of spiritual authority. Our effectiveness in ministry is dependent on understanding spiritual authority. Ministry makes us a target for the enemy and also opens us to the more severe dealings of God. Misuse of authority will bring judgment, surely and swiftly.

WHAT IS SPIRITUAL AUTHORITY?

We have added the word spiritual as a distinction from secular or natural authority. However, Romans 13:1-5 tells us that all authority is from God. Any real authority has its origin in God. That means that God also gives and removes authority to and from people both in the secular environment and in the spiritual. We always get the authority that we deserve.

When the children of Israel told Samuel that they wanted a King like the other nations, Samuel thought that they were rejecting him. However, God said no, that they were not rejecting Samuel but were rejecting Him. Samuel told them what a king would do to them. They still wanted one, anyway. This is a classic picture of Israel as a hypocrite. They wanted to look like the other nations but still call themselves the people of God. We can't act and look like the world and still walk under God's authority.

God's authority can't be separated from His rulership. Jesus said that all authority in Heaven and earth had been given to Him. He is the King of the Kingdom of God. He delegates that authority to whom it pleases Him. As believers we all have a measure of authority because we are "in the Name of Jesus". We speak the command of the King to demons and they have to flee. We speak to diseases and they are healed. All done by the authority of the Name of Jesus.

As we continue with Jesus we come under authority—His delegated spiritual authority. The Kingdom of God is structured. The Church is structured. All things are ordered of God. We submit or resist.

We have confused "direct authority" with "delegated authority". By direct authority, I mean our access to God as priests. We have direct access by the Blood of Jesus. We petition God and He answers. We have the right to use the Name of Jesus. We even receive revelation directly. However, this doesn't mean that as we mature, we have no need of anyone else. God doesn't intend that we always receive from Him directly; but teaches us our need of each other by bringing His word to us through some of His servants.

Matthew 10:40-42 NASB

(40) "He who receives you receives Me, and he who receives Me receives Him who sent Me.

(41) "He who receives a prophet in *the* name of a prophet shall receive a prophet's reward; and he who receives a righteous man in the name of a righteous man shall receive a righteous man's reward.

(42) "And whoever in the name of a disciple gives to one of these little ones even a cup of cold water to drink, truly I say to you, he shall not lose his reward."

Luke 10:16 NASB

(16) "The one who listens to you listens to Me, and the one who rejects you rejects Me; and he who rejects Me rejects the One who sent Me."

As we see from these scriptures, God places Himself one step behind His delegated authority. The attitude with which we receive God's representatives is also applied to the way we receive God. He says that the way we treat His delegated authority is the way we treat Him. We see this clearly with the Apostle Paul.

Acts 9:5-6 NASB

(5) And he said, "Who are You, Lord?" And He *said,* "I am Jesus whom you are persecuting,

(6) but get up and enter the city, and it will be told you what you must do."

During his encounter on the road to Damascus, it would have been easy for Jesus to tell him everything that was needed. Instead, Jesus tells him to go to the city and he would be told what to do. Paul does this and Ananias, a simple believer, comes and lays hands on Paul for him to receive his sight and the Holy Spirit. Why did Jesus do it this way? Why involve Ananias? Because, Paul encountered spiritual authority on the Damascus road, and his submission was tested by his receiving from Ananias.

The Lord has determined that there are some things that we will never receive from Him unless we can receive from His delegated authority. Thus, we stay dependent on each other in the Lord.

1 Corinthians 12:21-25 NASB

(21) And the eye cannot say to the hand, "I have no need of you"; or again the head to the feet, "I have no need of you."

(22) On the contrary, it is much truer that the members of the body which seem to be weaker are necessary;

(23) and those *members* of the body which we deem less honorable, on these we bestow more abundant honor, and our less presentable members become much more presentable,

(24) whereas our more presentable members have no need *of it*. But God has *so* composed the body, giving more abundant honor to that *member* which lacked,

(25) so that there may be no division in the body, but *that* the members may have the same care for one another.

THE PRINCIPLE OF AUTHORITY

God's authority represents God Himself; whereas, His power represents His acts. Many times we seek after the power of God so that mighty acts might be done, but forget about His authority. Usually this is done out of ignorance of God and His ways, however, sometimes it is done out of rebellion because a person is unwilling to come under authority. You can't have authority without being under authority. Authority flows from the Throne of God to His creation in an orderly manner.

Matthew 8:7-10 NASB

(7) Jesus *said to him, "I will come and heal him."

(8) But the centurion said, "Lord, I am not worthy for You to come under my roof, but just say the word, and my servant will be healed.

(9) "For I also am a man under authority, with soldiers under me; and I say to this one, 'Go!' and he goes, and to another, 'Come!' and he comes, and to my slave, 'Do this!' and he does *it*."

(10) Now when Jesus heard *this,* He marveled and said to those who were following, "Truly I say to you, I have not found such great faith with anyone in Israel.

The centurion said that he was one *under* authority not one *of* authority. When one is under authority, one can recognize authority and knows the necessity of obedience to the word of authority or suffer the consequences. As seen here, recognition of authority provides faith.

The Centurion recognized that Jesus walked in spiritual authority. That was why Jesus had only to speak the word and He would be obeyed. The Centurion understood this because, he too, walked in *governmental authority* and could, by a word, direct those for whom he was responsible.

I have seen these scriptures twisted and used to justify a worldly authority of "lording it over" (which Jesus condemned). The "shepherding movement" used these verses to emphasize that the Centurion was "a man under authority" and used this to say that we all must be under authority to a "shepherd" and give obedience to him even if he was wrong (just as Sarah obeyed Abraham when he said she was his sister when they went to Egypt) trusting God to protect us from the shepherd's mistakes. They said that to "have authority" one must be "under authority", which, in the broadest sense is true; however, their application meant that one had to be "under" another person's (shepherd's) authority.

When the Centurion said that he was "a man under authority", he meant that he derived his authority from the *government* that he served. He didn't have authority because he was under an army commander. He had authority because he was part of the government's army. Had he left the army, none of those of whom he spoke would obey him anymore because he no longer had any *governmental authority*.

It is the same in the Kingdom of God. We exercise *governmental authority*, which is "loaned" to us as long as we live and work under His government. To exercise authority one must have the *right* to do so. To attempt to exercise authority without having the right to do it makes it *illegitimate* authority and puts it in the category of the world and the principle of Satan.

Another example of having authority when under governmental authority is Adam. God placed Adam under His authority and gave him a commandment (law) that he might learn obedience: "Do not eat of the tree in the midst of the Garden." Then, God gave Adam dominion (authority) over all of the created things. As long as Adam remained obedient under authority, he had governmental authority over everything else. When he sinned (disobeyed), he came out from under God's authority and lost his governmental authority over the created things.

God built into Adam the desire and ability to rule. However, He didn't intend for Adam to rule without Him but would rule as His delegate in the earth. Adam's rule over the living things on the earth would flow from his fellowship with God and understanding of His purposes.

When Adam fell, the *desire* to rule was still inherent in him, however, he lost the *ability* to rule in a godly manner. This is what he passed to the generations that followed.

There was also another aspect of Adam's rulership. Because he ruled before the fall as a delegate of God, there is also inherent in Adam's descendants the need to be ruled as God ruled Adam.

The Principle of Satan

Because of the fall of Adam, natural authority is *taken* rather than *given*. Because it is exercised without the fellowship of God it is of the same nature as the authority exercised by Satan.

Before he became Satan, Lucifer, at some point, decided that he would *take* authority over all, even God.

Isaiah 14:12-14 NASB
> (12) "How you have fallen from heaven, O star of the morning, son of the dawn! You have been cut down to the earth, You who have weakened the nations!

> (13) "But you said in your heart, 'I will ascend to heaven; I will raise my throne above the stars of God, And I will sit on the mount of assembly In the recesses of the north.

> (14) 'I will ascend above the heights of the clouds; I will make myself like the Most High.'

The taking of authority is a principle of Satan and is directly opposed to the principle of authority exemplified by the Lord Jesus. It is possible in our work to stand with Christ in terms of doctrine and, yet, stand with Satan in terms of authority.

Pride caused Lucifer to desire to usurp God's authority—to ascend to His Throne. The result was that Lucifer became Satan and now desires to overthrow all submission to God's authority. This is Satan's Primary Principle—stand against God's authority (resist).

It is pride within us that causes us to harbor within our hearts this same principle of Satan. Yet, the scriptures say that "God resists the proud but gives grace to the humble" (1 Peter 5:5). You see, if we "stand against God's authority", God "stands against us". However, Jesus showed us how to "stand under God's authority" (submit).

Philippians 2:5-8 NASB

(5) Have this attitude in yourselves which was also in Christ Jesus,

(6) who, although He existed in the form of God, did not regard equality with God a thing to be grasped,

(7) but emptied Himself, taking the form of a bond-servant, *and* being made in the likeness of men.

(8) Being found in appearance as a man, He humbled Himself by becoming obedient to the point of death, even death on a cross.

To serve without orders in disobedience to authority will result in God's judgment. Nadab and Abihu offered "strange fire" (unauthorized fire) to the Lord. They were the sons of Aaron which meant that they had helped with the offerings many times. They had seen Aaron perform the offering rituals and probably didn't see anything too difficult in them. As a consequence, since they felt like they were perfectly capable to doing the offering, they did one without realizing that only Aaron had to authority (the right and the responsibility) for offerings. God had delegated this to him. Because they lacked understanding about God's delegated authority, they suffered the consequences.

Leviticus 10:1-2 NASB

(1) Now Nadab and Abihu, the sons of Aaron, took their respective firepans, and after putting fire in them, placed incense on it and offered strange fire before the LORD, which He had not commanded them.

(2) And fire came out from the presence of the LORD and consumed them, and they died before the LORD.

Another way that the principle of Satan is manifested in us is in our desire to find fault. We try to find fault with the authority over us so that we won't have to submit. This fault-finding attitude is revealed by our mouths. The scripture says that "out of the abundance of the heart the mouth speaketh". When this touches God's authority (delegated or otherwise), it produces trouble for us.

Numbers 12:1-2 NASB

(1) Then Miriam and Aaron spoke against Moses because of the Cushite woman whom he had married (for he had married a Cushite woman);

(2) and they said, "Has the LORD indeed spoken only through Moses? Has He not spoken through us as well?" And the LORD heard it.

God heard the grumbling and brought judgment immediately. His presence left the tent of meeting and Miriam's leprosy caused her to be cut off from the congregation for 7 days and the people had to wait until this rebellion issue was cleared before they could move on.

Even though Miriam spoke too much, she didn't let her mouth overload her the way Korah did. He went beyond rebellion and also reviled the Lord's authority.

Numbers 16:1-3 NASB

(1) Now Korah the son of Izhar, the son of Kohath, the son of Levi, with Dathan and Abiram, the sons of Eliab, and On the son of Peleth, sons of Reuben, took *action,*

(2) and they rose up before Moses, together with some of the sons of Israel, two hundred and fifty leaders of the congregation, chosen in the assembly, men of renown.

(3) They assembled together against Moses and Aaron, and said to them, "You have gone far enough, for all the congregation are holy, every one of them, and the LORD is in their midst; so why do you exalt yourselves above the assembly of the LORD?"

Numbers 16:8-11 NASB

(8) Then Moses said to Korah, "Hear now, you sons of Levi,

(9) is it not enough for you that the God of Israel has separated you from the *rest of* the congregation of Israel, to bring you near to Himself, to do the service of the tabernacle of the LORD, and to stand before the congregation to minister to them;

(10) and that He has brought you near, *Korah,* and all your brothers, sons of Levi, with you? And are you seeking for the priesthood also?

(11) "Therefore you and all your company are gathered together against the LORD; but as for Aaron, who is he that you grumble against him?"

Numbers 16:12-14 NASB

(12) Then Moses sent a summons to Dathan and Abiram, the sons of Eliab; but they said, "We will not come up.

(13) "Is it not enough that you have brought us up out of a land flowing with milk and honey to have us die in the wilderness, but you would also lord it over us?

(14) "Indeed, you have not brought us into a land flowing with milk and honey, nor have you given us an inheritance of fields and vineyards. Would you put out the eyes of these men? We will not come up!"

Numbers 16:28-33 NASB

(28) Moses said, "By this you shall know that the LORD has sent me to do all these deeds; for this is not my doing.

(29) "If these men die the death of all men or if they suffer the fate of all men, *then* the LORD has not sent me.

(30) "But if the LORD brings about an entirely new thing and the ground opens its mouth and swallows them up with all that is theirs, and they descend alive into Sheol, then you will understand that these men have spurned the LORD."

(31) As he finished speaking all these words, the ground that was under them split open;

(32) and the earth opened its mouth and swallowed them up, and their households, and all the men who belonged to Korah with *their* possessions.

(33) So they and all that belonged to them went down alive to Sheol; and the earth closed over them, and they perished from the midst of the assembly.

God and His delegated authority are inseparable. You can't reject God's representative on the one hand and receive God on the other. God jealousy protects His authority. 10 times the children of Israel tempted God; 5 times they disbelieved Him; yet God forebore and forgave. But, for this rebellion, God came to judge.

They went alive into the pit (sheol, hell). Even though the gates of hell shall not prevail against the Church, a rebellious spirit can open the gates of hell. Many times the Church doesn't prevail because there is rebellion in its midst. All sin releases the power of death, but rebellion releases it the most.

King David, a man after the Lord's own heart, exemplifies the proper attitude toward God's authority. Saul was anointed King over Israel when the people demanded a king. Saul disobeyed the commandment of the Lord in the matter of King Agag and, as a consequence was rejected by God as king. David is then anointed king by Samuel. Now, David has a problem. He is the new anointed king, but Saul still sits on the throne. Saul has not descended from the Kingship and David has not ascended.

Saul seeks to kill David because he knows that David is to be the new king. What is David to do? Should he take matters into his own hand and remove Saul?

1 Samuel 24:3-7 NASB

(3) He came to the sheepfolds on the way, where there *was* a cave; and Saul went in to relieve himself. Now David and his men were sitting in the inner recesses of the cave.

(4) The men of David said to him, "Behold, *this is* the day of which the LORD said to you, 'Behold; I am about to give your enemy into your hand, and you shall do to him as it seems good to you.'" Then David arose and cut off the edge of Saul's robe secretly.

(5) It came about afterward that David's conscience bothered him because he had cut off the edge of Saul's *robe.*

(6) So he said to his men, "Far be it from me because of the LORD that I should do this thing to my lord, the LORD'S anointed, to stretch out my hand against him, since he is the LORD'S anointed."

(7) David persuaded his men with *these* words and did not allow them to rise up against Saul. And Saul arose, left the cave, and went on *his* way.

David refused to act in rebellion. He refused to raise his hand against the Lord's anointed. Even cutting off the hem of the skirt caused guilt. Later, another test was offered to David.

1 Samuel 26:8-11 NASB

(8) Then Abishai said to David, "Today God has delivered your enemy into your hand; now therefore, please let me strike him with the spear to the ground with one stroke, and I will not strike him the second time."

(9) But David said to Abishai, "Do not destroy him, for who can stretch out his hand against the LORD'S anointed and be without guilt?"

(10) David also said, "As the LORD lives, surely the LORD will strike him, or his day will come that he dies, or he will go down into battle and perish.

(11) "The LORD forbid that I should stretch out my hand against the LORD'S anointed; but now please take the spear that is at his head and the jug of water, and let us go."

Even when others are telling him that it is the Lord's will to kill Saul, David refuses to lift his hand against the Lord's anointed. Like David we need to remember that we are in subjection not to the man but to the anointing that is on the man. The same anointing that came when God gave him as His delegated authority. David so respected this that later, he even had the man killed that killed Saul (2 Samuel 1:14-16)!

NATURAL AND SPIRITUAL AUTHORITY

There are two types of authority—natural and spiritual. All authority whether natural or spiritual is derived from our relationships. The natural authority in a family is derived from God's order and structure and our relationship to it. Spiritual authority is derived from our relationship with the Lord and the work that we are called to in Him. All authority relates to responsibility. If we have responsibility, we have authority and vice versa.

I have authority in my family because I am the husband of my wife and the father of my children. Because they are related to me, they are subject to my authority. They are not subject because I am good or wise but because God established it that way. My family doesn't have to decide to be subject or not. They are subject by being my family. (They do have to decide about obedience-- remember, submission is absolute, but obedience is conditional.)

The same is true of our authority in the Family of God. The authority of the believer is based on the fact that one has a relationship with Jesus Christ and, therefore, with the Father. It is based on who Christ is and on who we are in Christ.

God has chosen (by His own design) in the family to set the husband as representative of Christ and the wife as representative of the Church. It is difficult for the wife to submit to her husband until she can see the delegated authority vested in him. The real issue is God's authority not her husband.

1 Corinthians 11:3 NASB

(3) But I want you to understand that Christ is the head of every man, and the man is the head of a woman, and God is the head of Christ.

This is God's ordained structure. We have to fit into it whether we like it or not. Again, we have the choice to "stand under" or "stand against".

Ephesians 5:22-24 NASB

(22) Wives, *be subject* to your own husbands, as to the Lord.

(23) For the husband is the head of the wife, as Christ also is the head of the church, He Himself *being* the Savior of the body.

(24) But as the church is subject to Christ, so also the wives *ought to be* to their husbands in everything.

Colossians 3:18 NASB

(18) Wives, be subject to your husbands, as is fitting in the Lord.

1 Peter 3:1-2 NASB

(1) In the same way, you wives, be submissive to your own husbands so that even if any *of them* are disobedient to the word, they may be won without a word by the behavior of their wives,

(2) as they observe your chaste and respectful behavior.

Because of their relational submission to their own husbands, women are restricted in the broader range of authority that is available to them.

1 Timothy 2:12-14 NASB

(12) But I do not allow a woman to teach or exercise authority over a man, but to remain quiet.

(13) For it was Adam who was first created, *and* then Eve.

(14) And *it was* not Adam *who* was deceived, but the woman being deceived, fell into transgression.

1 Corinthians 14:34-35 NASB

(34) The women are to keep silent in the churches; for they are not permitted to speak, but are to subject themselves, just as the Law also says.

(35) If they desire to learn anything, let them ask their own husbands at home; for it is improper for a woman to speak in church.

Within the Church, the woman is not to have the position of teacher over men. This is not to say that a woman cannot testify, share, or otherwise proclaim Jesus. Women may even teach, but the parameters of their teaching is limited by the scriptures.

Titus 2:3-5 NASB

(3) Older women likewise are to be reverent in their behavior, not malicious gossips nor enslaved to much wine, teaching what is good,

(4) so that they may encourage the young women to love their husbands, to love their children,

(5) *to be* sensible, pure, workers at home, kind, being subject to their own husbands, so that

the word of God will not be dishonored.

While leadership is primarily a man's responsibly, under proper male covering and headship, women can conduct powerful effective ministries. Spiritual authority comes with the anointing of the Holy Spirit. Leadership within a believers' gathering flows with the anointing. As the Holy Spirit brings forth His gifts through various people, both men and women, the spiritual authority flows from person to person, also.

Women can:

➢ Receive and minister spiritual gifts (Acts 21:8,9)

➢ Teach the younger women (Titus 2:3-5)

➢ Minister hospitality to ministers (Roman 16:1-2)

➢ Share in an almost unlimited ministry under the covering and company of their husbands. (Acts 18:1-3 18,26)

None of this is a question of inferiority or of value. Men and women are of equal worth, but have different functions in the Lord. Different functions require different responsibilities. Since responsibility is linked to authority, different functions require different aspects of authority.

Children too are under the authority of the parents. Again, this is not a decision that is made but is due to the fact that they are the children of the parents.

Ephesians 6:1-3 NASB
(1) Children, obey your parents in the Lord, for this is right.

(2) HONOR YOUR FATHER AND MOTHER (which is the first commandment with a promise),

(3) SO THAT IT MAY BE WELL WITH YOU, AND THAT YOU MAY LIVE LONG ON THE EARTH.

Colossians 3:20 NASB
(20) Children, be obedient to your parents in all things, for this is well-pleasing to the Lord.

This is a principle that also carries over into our Church family relationships.

1 Peter 5:5 NASB
(5) You younger men, likewise, be subject to *your* elders; and all of you, clothe yourselves with humility toward one another, for GOD IS OPPOSED TO THE PROUD, BUT GIVES GRACE TO THE HUMBLE.

This naturally leads us into relational authority in the Church for we are admonished to honor those that have authority over us.

1 Thessalonians 5:12-13 NASB
(12) But we request of you, brethren, that you appreciate those who diligently labor among you, and have charge over you in the Lord and give you instruction,

(13) and that you esteem them very highly in love because of their work. Live in peace with one another.

CONFLICT OF AUTHORITY

All spiritual authority has its basis in God and is received from God. It cannot be taken but only received as God gives it to us. Jesus did not take authority but received it from the Father.

Matthew 28:18 NASB

(18) And Jesus came up and spoke to them, saying, "All authority has been given to Me in heaven and on earth.

When the Father made Jesus both Lord and King, He became the ruler of the Kingdom of God and it is from His position as King that He exercises authority.

1 Corinthians 15:24 NASB

(24) then *comes* the end, when He hands over the kingdom to the God and Father, when He has abolished all rule and all authority and power.

Since Jesus has all authority, what authority is He abolishing in His Kingdom? He is abolishing all natural, positional, secular authority that has been taken under the principle of Satan without regard to God.

Jesus clearly warned us of the difference between the authority of the world and His authority.

Matthew 20:25-28 NASB

(25) But Jesus called them to Himself and said, "You know that the rulers of the Gentiles lord it over them, and *their* great men exercise authority over them.

(26) "It is not this way among you, but whoever wishes to become great among you shall be your servant,

(27) and whoever wishes to be first among you shall be your slave;

(28) just as the Son of Man did not come to be served, but to serve, and to give His life a ransom for many."

Jesus clearly contrasts the way the world handles authority and the way that we should as His followers. Spiritual authority has nothing to do with being great or exercising authority over people but instead is service to others. Natural or worldly authority seeks to be served and exercise authority over as many people as possible, whereas spiritual authority seeks to serve others and never seeks to exercise authority over people.

Authority Over What?

In the Church today, many speak of having authority over some number of people or some number of churches or some number of ministries. But, is this what Jesus had in mind?

Jesus gave very specific authority to the disciples:

Matthew 10:1 NASB
   (1) Jesus summoned His twelve disciples and gave them authority over unclean spirits, to cast them out, and to heal every kind of disease and every kind of sickness.

This is clear. The disciples were given authority over unclean spirits and every kind of disease and sickness.

When Jesus sent them out in pairs, He, again, gave very specific authority to them.

Luke 9:1-2 NASB
   (1) And He called the twelve together, and gave them power and authority over all the demons and to heal diseases.

   (2) And He sent them out to proclaim the kingdom of God and to perform healing.

Again, it is clear: authority over all demons and to heal disease. And, the purpose for which the authority was given is also very clear: to proclaim the Kingdom of God and to perform healing.

They were given authority by Jesus to proclaim and to perform the purposes of the King.

When Jesus sent out the seventy, they were only directed according to the plan of the Lord. They weren't sent to just anyplace but only to the places where He was coming.

Luke 10:1 NASB
   (1) Now after this the Lord appointed seventy others, and sent them in pairs ahead of Him to every city and place where He Himself was going to come.

When they returned and were excited about the fact that the demons were subject to them, Jesus told them why:

Luke 10:19 NASB
   (19) "Behold, I have given you authority to tread on serpents and scorpions, and over all the power of the enemy, and nothing will injure you.

Notice that in all of these cases, Jesus gave authority over spiritual things such as demons and sicknesses but never gave any of them authority over people. Likewise, Jesus has given us authority over all of the power of the enemy so that we might overcome but the scriptures say specifically that we don't wrestle with flesh and blood, that is, people. It would seem to me that so many in the Church have it backwards. They want to exercise authority over people but have very little authority in spiritual matters.

Only One has been given authority over people and that One is Jesus.

John 17:1-2 NASB
   (1) Jesus spoke these things; and lifting up His eyes to heaven, He said, "Father, the hour has come; glorify Your Son, that the Son may glorify You,

   (2) even as You gave Him authority over all flesh, that to all whom You have given Him, He

may give eternal life.

We function as the "under guardians and managers" of the "heirs of salvation" until they come of age and function as sons. Paul speaks of this when he speaks of the authority given to him.

2 Corinthians 10:8 NASB

> (8) For even if I boast somewhat further about our authority, which the Lord gave for building you up and not for destroying you, I will not be put to shame,

2 Corinthians 13:10 NASB

> (10) For this reason I am writing these things while absent, so that when present I *need* not use severity, in accordance with the authority which the Lord gave me for building up and not for tearing down.

So, we see that when it comes to people, even Paul's authority was limited to the specific purposes of the Lord for building up. This had to do with the apostolic work of the Kingdom and Paul's function as a "master builder". We are given spiritual authority to fulfill the function of our calling and to accomplish the work that the Lord has assigned.

Application of Spiritual Authority

The crucial aspect of spiritual authority is how it is applied within the Church. The problem that has occurred previously is that our application of authority has been based on our understanding of authority as being over people (authority applied according to the World's principles). Let's look at the scriptures with the understanding of authority as service; that it relates to function; and that leadership is by example.

Jesus repeatedly expressed authority in terms of example, responsibility, and function by using the picture of shepherds and sheep. Shepherds lead sheep by going in front, never by driving them from behind.

We think of "being in charge" as having the authority to order people around. This is not the way Jesus thought of "being in charge".

Luke 12:42 NASB

> (42) And the Lord said, "Who then is the faithful and sensible steward, whom his master will put in charge of his servants, to give them their rations at the proper time?

In this scripture being "in charge" dealt with function and the responsibility of providing food, not with the authority to order people around. We also see this concept applied by Paul.

1 Thessalonians 5:12 NASB

> (12) But we request of you, brethren, that you appreciate those who diligently labor among you, and have charge over you in the Lord and give you instruction,

In this scripture having "charge over you" relates to function and their responsibility is to give instruction (food). Again, this has nothing to do with ordering people around.

Of course, the scripture that is quoted by those who think of authority as a position with the right to demand obedience is I Timothy 5:17:

1 Timothy 5:17 NASB
> (17) The elders who rule well are to be considered worthy of double honor, especially those who work hard at preaching and teaching.

They emphasize the word "rule" as in "I'm top dog and its my way or the highway". However, the word translated as rule means "to go in front", "lead" (sounds like a shepherd's job, doesn't it?). This word is also translated as "manage".

The one who goes in front is to be our example as we look at their conduct and faith.

Hebrews 13:7 NASB
> (7) Remember those who led you, who spoke the word of God to you; and considering the result of their conduct, imitate their faith.

This is why we can offer obedience and submission. We are being obedient and submissive to the Lord in them and to the job function that the Lord has given them. They must give an account to the Lord concerning their conduct toward their job responsibilities.

Hebrews 13:17 NASB
> (17) Obey your leaders and submit *to them,* for they keep watch over your souls as those <u>who will give an account</u>. Let them do this with joy and not with grief, for this would be unprofitable for you.

They keep watch over our souls just like a shepherd keeps watch over the flock and are responsible to God for this function.

It is interesting that the New American Standard Bible translates "rule" as manage when speaking of the requirements for Overseers and Deacons as discussed in 1 Timothy chapter 3.

The idea of managing is probably closer to the intended meaning of the use of the word "rule". We understand that we manage that for which we are responsible. A department manager in a business only has authority over the business functions and how people relate to the necessities of operations. The manager has no authority over the employees for non-job related conduct except as it affects job performance.

The Overseers or elders of the Church go before the people to lead by example and conduct in order to provide instruction and manage the flock. They are held accountable by the Lord for how they perform these functions. We are to submit to the Lord in them and obey His instructions through them as they walk in governmental authority.

The Church, like the Children of Israel when they told Samuel that they wanted a king, has rejected the government of the Kingdom for the government of the World System. Worldly authority only takes and keeps on taking until all are in servitude to it; whereas, spiritual authority serves like a father serves his family, building them up and desiring for them fulfill their purpose.

There are no "offices" in the Church. Only servant-leaders called of God to function according to His plan and purpose for the completion of the work fore-ordained for them that many sons might be brought to glory that God may be all in all.

Date _____

Scripture _____

● Vision _____ ● Prophecy _____ ● Revelation _____

(Circle One)

_____

_____

_____

_____

_____

_____

_____

_____

_____

_____

_____

_____

_____

_____

_____

_____

Date _____

Scripture _____

● Vision _____ ● Prophecy _____ ● Revelation _____

(Circle One)

_____

_____

_____

_____

_____

_____

_____

_____

_____

_____

_____

_____

_____

_____

Date _____

Scripture _____

● Vision _____ ● Prophecy _____ ● Revelation _____
(Circle One)

_____

_____

_____

_____

_____

_____

_____

_____

_____

_____

_____

_____

_____

_____

Date _____

Scripture _____

● Vision _____ ● Prophecy _____ ● Revelation _____

(Circle One)

_____

_____

_____

_____

_____

_____

_____

_____

_____

_____

_____

_____

_____

_____

Date _____

Scripture _____

● Vision _____   ● Prophecy _____   ● Revelation _____

(Circle One)

_____

_____

_____

_____

_____

_____

_____

_____

_____

_____

_____

_____

_____

_____

Date _____

Scripture _____

● Vision _____ ● Prophecy _____ ● Revelation _____

(Circle One)

_____

_____

_____

_____

_____

_____

_____

_____

_____

_____

_____

_____

_____

Date _____

Scripture _____

● Vision _____ ● Prophecy _____ ● Revelation _____

(Circle One)

_____

_____

_____

_____

_____

_____

_____

_____

_____

_____

_____

_____

_____

_____

Date _____

Scripture _____

● Vision _____ ● Prophecy _____ ● Revelation _____

(Circle One)

_____

_____

_____

_____

_____

_____

_____

_____

_____

_____

_____

_____

_____

_____

DECREE FOR JUSTICE IN RELATIONSHIPS
Ryan Lestrange

Proverbs 13:20- He who walks with wise men will be wise,
But the companion of fools will suffer harm.

I decree the justice of God over my relationships! Justice over relationships with spiritual leaders. Justice over relationships with friends. Justice over relationships with family and loved ones. I pray for the exposure of every demon of strife, deception and evil lies concerning the relationships in my life. I refuse to give in to the accusations of the enemy. I say that I am quick to forgive and have the mind of Christ. I release the power of the blood of Jesus over my relationships and confess that I will not be divided from those God has assigned to my life.

Date _____

Scripture _____

● Vision _____   ● Prophecy _____   ● Revelation _____

(Circle One)

_____

_____

_____

_____

_____

_____

_____

_____

_____

_____

_____

_____

_____

_____

Date _____

Scripture _____

● Vision _____ ● Prophecy _____ ● Revelation _____

(Circle One)

_____

_____

_____

_____

_____

_____

_____

_____

_____

_____

_____

_____

_____

Date _____

Scripture _____

● Vision _____   ● Prophecy _____   ● Revelation _____
(Circle One)

_____

_____

_____

_____

_____

_____

_____

_____

_____

_____

_____

_____

_____

_____

Date _____

Scripture _____

● Vision _____ ● Prophecy _____ ● Revelation _____

(Circle One)

_____

_____

_____

_____

_____

_____

_____

_____

_____

_____

_____

_____

_____

_____

Date _____

Scripture _____

● Vision _____   ● Prophecy _____   ● Revelation _____

(Circle One)

_____

_____

_____

_____

_____

_____

_____

_____

_____

_____

_____

_____

_____

_____

_____

_____

Date _____

Scripture _____

● Vision _____ ● Prophecy _____ ● Revelation _____

(Circle One)

_____

_____

_____

_____

_____

_____

_____

_____

_____

_____

_____

_____

_____

_____

_____

_____

Date _____

Scripture _____

● Vision _____ ● Prophecy _____ ● Revelation _____

(Circle One)

_____

_____

_____

_____

_____

_____

_____

_____

_____

_____

_____

_____

_____

_____

_____

_____

_____

Date _____

Scripture _____

• Vision _____   • Prophecy _____   • Revelation _____

(Circle One)

_____

_____

_____

_____

_____

_____

_____

_____

_____

_____

_____

_____

_____

_____

_____

Scripture

● Vision   ● Prophecy   ● Revelation

(Circle One)

Scripture

Date _____

Scripture _____

● Vision _____ ● Prophecy _____ ● Revelation _____

(Circle One)

_____

_____

_____

_____

_____

_____

_____

_____

_____

_____

_____

_____

_____

_____

Date _____

Scripture _____

● Vision _____ ● Prophecy _____ ● Revelation _____

(Circle One)

_____
_____
_____
_____
_____
_____
_____
_____
_____
_____
_____
_____
_____
_____
_____
_____

Date _____

Scripture _____

● Vision _____ ● Prophecy _____ ● Revelation _____
                                              (Circle One)

_____

_____

_____

_____

_____

_____

_____

_____

_____

_____

_____

_____

_____

● Vision _____   ● Prophecy _____   ● Revelation _____

(Circle One)

_____

_____

_____

_____

_____

_____

_____

_____

_____

_____

_____

_____

_____

_____

_____

Date _____

Scripture _____

● Vision _____ ● Prophecy _____ ● Revelation _____

(Circle One)

_____

_____

_____

_____

_____

_____

_____

_____

_____

_____

_____

_____

_____

_____

Date _____

Scripture _____

● Vision _____ ● Prophecy _____ ● Revelation _____
(Circle One)

_____
_____
_____
_____
_____
_____
_____
_____
_____
_____
_____
_____
_____

Date _____

Scripture _____

● Vision _____ ● Prophecy _____ ● Revelation _____
(Circle One)

_____

_____

_____

_____

_____

_____

_____

_____

_____

_____

_____

_____

_____

_____

Date _____

Scripture _____

● Vision _____ ● Prophecy _____ ● Revelation _____

(Circle One)

_____

_____

_____

_____

_____

_____

_____

_____

_____

_____

_____

_____

_____

_____

Prophetic Word

Jamie Rohrbaugh - January 17, 2019

I heard the Lord say, "I am giving out new mantles of intercession!"

In this season, many who have felt their intercessory fires die out because of fatigue, burnout, and injury will find themselves suddenly pulled back into fiery intercession—the likes of which they had feared were lost to them.

These intercessors will be surprised when these new mantles of intercession come, for they will be at higher levels than each intercessor has experienced before. For example, whereas previously an intercessor was anointed to pray for a church, now they will be anointed to pray with burden for a nation.

Some intercessors who have previously had keen insight will find their insight renewed and sharpened. Others who struggled with a lack of insight before will suddenly have the insight they need. It will be a gift from the Lord.

I saw a vision of an eagle, high on a rock in a lonely place, being renewed.

The eagle, who was used to mastering the sky, had developed crust on his beak and his feathers were in rough shape. He had drawn away to this high but lonely place to be renewed.

In this vision, I saw the hand of the Lord reach out of Heaven and personally preen the eagle's feathers. Wherever He touched, new life sprang up. New feathers formed.

Then I saw the Lord grasp the eagle's head in the palm of His hand and flick off the crust from his beak with His fingers. As He did, tears fell from the eagle's eyes. The eagle had expected to have to clean himself, but the loving hand of the Creator did it for him. It felt too good to be true. Then I saw the Lord lift the eagle in His hand and open His palm, releasing him back to the sky. The eagle hesitated, not sure if it was really okay for him to fly again. But the Lord gently launched the eagle out into the sky.

When the bird took flight, he noticed that his wings were stronger. His vision was clearer. His body was stronger, and once again he was master of the skies.

Some of you have felt like that eagle.

You have been worn out. Weary and fatigued, you have been in a lonely place with no one around. You have felt like you have lost your vision. Sometimes, you have wondered if you have lost your anointing too.

But the Lord says to you today:

"This day, I am repairing your feathers. I am healing your heart, and I am restoring your vision. I am going to launch you into mastery of all you survey again, and you will function better there than ever before."

The Lord is going to unite your heart after His purposes once more. He is filling you with fresh intercessory fire. His hand is upon you, even in your lonely place.

Fear not, little ones. It is the Father's good pleasure to give you the Kingdom. He has not brought you this far to abandon you. Instead, He is re-firing you and returning you to the skies.

Date _____

Scripture _____

● Vision _____ ● Prophecy _____ ● Revelation _____

(Circle One)

_____

_____

_____

_____

_____

_____

_____

_____

_____

_____

_____

_____

_____

_____

Date _____

Scripture _____

● Vision _____ ● Prophecy _____ ● Revelation _____

(Circle One)

_____

_____

_____

_____

_____

_____

_____

_____

_____

_____

_____

_____

_____

_____

_____

_____

Date _____

Scripture _____

● Vision _____ ● Prophecy _____ ● Revelation _____

(Circle One)

_____

_____

_____

_____

_____

_____

_____

_____

_____

_____

_____

_____

_____

_____

Date _____

Scripture _____

● Vision _____ ● Prophecy _____ ● Revelation _____

(Circle One)

_____

_____

_____

_____

_____

_____

_____

_____

_____

_____

_____

_____

_____

_____

Date _____

Scripture _____

● Vision _____   ● Prophecy _____   ● Revelation _____

(Circle One)

_____

_____

_____

_____

_____

_____

_____

_____

_____

_____

_____

_____

_____

_____

_____

_____

Date _____

Scripture _____

● Vision _____ ● Prophecy _____ ● Revelation _____

(Circle One)

_____

_____

_____

_____

_____

_____

_____

_____

_____

_____

_____

_____

_____

_____

_____

Date _____

Scripture _____

● Vision _____   ● Prophecy _____   ● Revelation _____
(Circle One)

_____
_____
_____
_____
_____
_____
_____
_____
_____
_____
_____
_____
_____
_____

Date _____

Scripture _____

● Vision _____ ● Prophecy _____ ● Revelation _____

(Circle One)

_____

_____

_____

_____

_____

_____

_____

_____

_____

_____

_____

_____

_____

Power of Prayer

A Serial Killer Caught
(excerpt from the book "Authority to Thread" Rebecca Greenwood)

A serial killer was on the loose in the city of Houston. He had murdered four individuals and the police had no leads. Spirits of fear and death were beginning to grip the city.

During prayer at church one night, we focused on the capture of the serial killer. We began to pray that the police would be led supernaturally to the killer. We prayeed that fear and death would not have access to the city. We declared that this terrorizing would come to an end and that he would be caught that evening.

When I arrived home, I quickly turned on the television to hear the breaking news at the top of the hour I heard the annoucer state that the police had received a phone call leading them to the killer and that he had been arrested. The call to the police came during the exact hour

Date _____

Scripture _____

● Vision _____ ● Prophecy _____ ● Revelation _____

(Circle One)

_____

_____

_____

_____

_____

_____

_____

_____

_____

_____

_____

_____

Date _____

Scripture _____

● Vision _____ ● Prophecy _____ ● Revelation _____
(Circle One)

_____

_____

_____

_____

_____

_____

_____

_____

_____

_____

_____

_____

_____

Date _____

Scripture _____

● Vision _____ ● Prophecy _____ ● Revelation _____

(Circle One)

_____

_____

_____

_____

_____

_____

_____

_____

_____

_____

_____

_____

_____

_____

Date _____

Scripture _____

● Vision _____   ● Prophecy _____   ● Revelation _____

(Circle One)

_____

_____

_____

_____

_____

_____

_____

_____

_____

_____

_____

_____

_____

_____

_____

Date _____

Scripture _____

● Vision _____ ● Prophecy _____ ● Revelation _____

(Circle One)

_____

_____

_____

_____

_____

_____

_____

_____

_____

_____

_____

_____

_____

Date _____

Scripture _____

● Vision _____ ● Prophecy _____ ● Revelation _____

(Circle One)

_____

_____

_____

_____

_____

_____

_____

_____

_____

_____

_____

_____

_____

Date _____

Scripture _____

● Vision _____ ● Prophecy _____ ● Revelation _____

(Circle One)

_____

_____

_____

_____

_____

_____

_____

_____

_____

_____

_____

_____

_____

Date _____

Scripture _____

● Vision _____   ● Prophecy _____   ● Revelation _____
                                                          (Circle One)

_____

_____

_____

_____

_____

_____

_____

_____

_____

_____

_____

_____

_____

_____

Date _____

Scripture _____

• Vision _____ • Prophecy _____ • Revelation _____
(Circle One)

_____

_____

_____

_____

_____

_____

_____

_____

_____

_____

_____

_____

_____

_____

_____

_____

Date _____

Scripture _____

● Vision _____   ● Prophecy _____   ● Revelation _____

(Circle One)

_____

_____

_____

_____

_____

_____

_____

_____

_____

_____

_____

_____

_____

_____

_____

_____

Date _____

Scripture _____

● Vision _____ ● Prophecy _____ ● Revelation _____

(Circle One)

_____

_____

_____

_____

_____

_____

_____

_____

_____

_____

_____

_____

_____

_____

_____

_____

Date _____

Scripture _____

● Vision _____   ● Prophecy _____   ● Revelation _____

(Circle One)

_____
_____
_____
_____
_____
_____
_____
_____
_____
_____
_____
_____
_____

63

Date _____

Scripture _____

● Vision _____   ● Prophecy _____   ● Revelation _____

(Circle One)

_____

_____

_____

_____

_____

_____

_____

_____

_____

_____

_____

_____

_____

_____

_____

Date _____

Scripture _____

● Vision _____   ● Prophecy _____   ● Revelation _____

(Circle One)

_____

_____

_____

_____

_____

_____

_____

_____

_____

_____

_____

_____

_____

_____

_____

_____

Date _____

Scripture _____

● Vision _____ ● Prophecy _____ ● Revelation _____

(Circle One)

_____

_____

_____

_____

_____

_____

_____

_____

_____

_____

_____

_____

Date _____

Scripture _____

- Vision _____ - Prophecy _____ - Revelation _____

(Circle One)

_____

_____

_____

_____

_____

_____

_____

_____

_____

_____

_____

_____

_____

_____

Date _____

Scripture _____

● Vision _____   ● Prophecy _____   ● Revelation _____

(Circle One)

_____

_____

_____

_____

_____

_____

_____

_____

_____

_____

_____

_____

_____

Date _____

Scripture _____

● Vision _____ ● Prophecy _____ ● Revelation _____

(Circle One)

_____

_____

_____

_____

_____

_____

_____

_____

_____

_____

_____

_____

_____

_____

_____

_____

Date _____

Scripture _____

● Vision _____ ● Prophecy _____ ● Revelation _____

(Circle One)

_____

_____

_____

_____

_____

_____

_____

_____

_____

_____

_____

_____

_____

_____

_____

_____

Date _____

Scripture _____

● Vision _____ ● Prophecy _____ ● Revelation _____

(Circle One)

_____

_____

_____

_____

_____

_____

_____

_____

_____

_____

_____

_____

_____

Date _____

Scripture _____

● Vision _____   ● Prophecy _____   ● Revelation _____

(Circle One)

_____

_____

_____

_____

_____

_____

_____

_____

_____

_____

_____

_____

_____

_____

_____

_____

Date _____

Scripture _____

• Vision _____   • Prophecy _____   • Revelation _____
(Circle One)

_____

_____

_____

_____

_____

_____

_____

_____

_____

_____

_____

_____

_____

Scripture _____

● Vision _____   ● Prophecy _____   ● Revelation _____

(Circle One)

_____

_____

_____

_____

_____

_____

_____

_____

_____

_____

_____

_____

_____

_____

_____

Date _____

Scripture _____

● Vision _____ ● Prophecy _____ ● Revelation _____

(Circle One)

_____

_____

_____

_____

_____

_____

_____

_____

_____

_____

_____

_____

_____

_____

_____

_____

Date _____

Scripture _____

● Vision _____   ● Prophecy _____   ● Revelation _____

(Circle One)

_____

_____

_____

_____

_____

_____

_____

_____

_____

_____

_____

_____

_____

_____

_____

_____

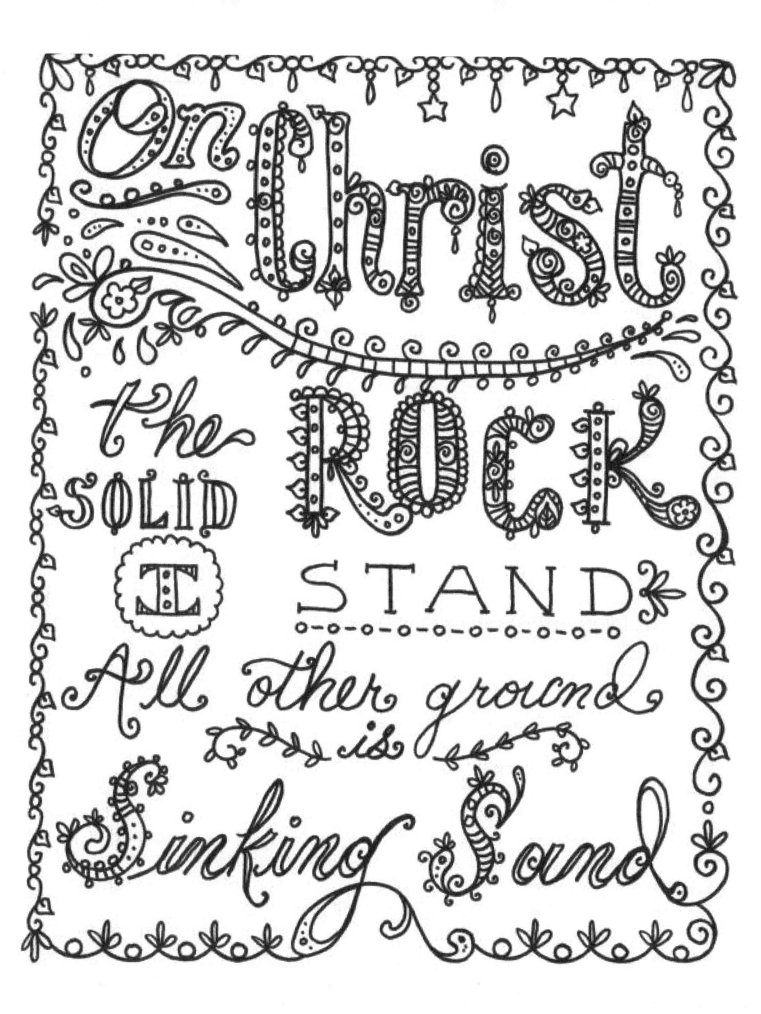

On Christ
The Rock
Solid

Stand

All other ground
is
Sinking Sand

Prophetic Word

by Dr. Judy Fornara - Spiritual Life Ministries

The Lord is gracious to His people in the earth and this year will be a sovereign year in the earth, showing the hand of God. There will be great storms and great suddenlies that show that the exalted God reigns in the earth.

North Dakota will greatly prosper this year because of her oil. American shall begin to spend more time and money on her own industry; a move for independence from Arab countries and China.

China will stay under the U.S.A. not above or beside her in greatness. Europe will give us trouble with all her socialism and Anti-Semitic ideas. Yet, they will stay subservient to the U.S.A.

America, your economy will stay strong this year and not go backwards because of your support for Israel. There shall be much shaking in the Middle East this year. Trump got out of Syria because of the evil of Russia's and Turkey's secret plans dominate the region. They will, together, give Israel much trouble, but my country (Israel) will always come out on top.

Korea must be revisited to make them know America is a dominate land that tells the truth and enforces the truth. The homosexual agenda wants to dominate the outlook of the church but I will cause them to lose ground this year, for my hand is still on the U.S.A.

The church will grow strong this year as more people will turn to Christ because of the pressures in the earth as we move towards the end of time.

A warrior spirit shall come alive in the church again this year. Pockets of prayer shall become popular this year for people to have breakthroughs in their lives in America.

Your worship shall increase with a new joy and move in the Spirit. The prophetic will come back more alive in America, and a hunger for the deeper things of God. People will want to press into God's Spirit to draw closer to His Spirit, so they know the mind of God for their lives. Healing will become more noticeable and more frequent in the church.

People will get hungry for the move of God not just playing church. The real anointing of God and deliverance will become more needed in the church. The power and encounters of God will be more manifested in the Body of Christ.

Hope will come alive again in the sovereign work of God who will show himself big for those who are righteous among the saints.

Date _____

Scripture _____

● Vision _____   ● Prophecy _____   ● Revelation _____
                                                              (Circle One)

_____

_____

_____

_____

_____

_____

_____

_____

_____

_____

_____

_____

_____

_____

Date _____

Scripture _____

● Vision _____   ● Prophecy _____   ● Revelation _____

(Circle One)

_____

_____

_____

_____

_____

_____

_____

_____

_____

_____

_____

_____

_____

_____

_____

Date _____

Scripture _____

● Vision _____ ● Prophecy _____ ● Revelation _____
(Circle One)

_____

_____

_____

_____

_____

_____

_____

_____

_____

_____

_____

_____

_____

_____

Date _____

Scripture _____

● Vision _____ ● Prophecy _____ ● Revelation _____

(Circle One)

_____

_____

_____

_____

_____

_____

_____

_____

_____

_____

_____

_____

_____

Date _____

Scripture _____

● Vision _____   ● Prophecy _____   ● Revelation _____
                                                    (Circle One)

_____

_____

_____

_____

_____

_____

_____

_____

_____

_____

_____

_____

_____

_____

_____

Date _____

Scripture _____

● Vision _____ ● Prophecy _____ ● Revelation _____

(Circle One)

_____

_____

_____

_____

_____

_____

_____

_____

_____

_____

_____

_____

_____

_____

_____

_____

Date _____

Scripture _____

● Vision _____ ● Prophecy _____ ● Revelation _____

(Circle One)

_____

_____

_____

_____

_____

_____

_____

_____

_____

_____

_____

_____

Date _____

Scripture _____

● Vision _____ ● Prophecy _____ ● Revelation _____

(Circle One)

_____

_____

_____

_____

_____

_____

_____

_____

_____

_____

_____

_____

_____

Date _____

Scripture _____

● Vision _____ ● Prophecy _____ ● Revelation _____
(Circle One)

_____

_____

_____

_____

_____

_____

_____

_____

_____

_____

_____

_____

_____

Date _____

Scripture _____

● Vision _____   ● Prophecy _____   ● Revelation _____
                                              (Circle One)

_____

_____

_____

_____

_____

_____

_____

_____

_____

_____

_____

_____

_____

Scripture _____

● Vision _____   ● Prophecy _____   ● Revelation _____

(Circle One)

_____

_____

_____

_____

_____

_____

_____

_____

_____

_____

_____

_____

_____

Date _____

Scripture _____

● Vision _____   ● Prophecy _____   ● Revelation _____

(Circle One)

_____

_____

_____

_____

_____

_____

_____

_____

_____

_____

_____

_____

_____

_____

_____

_____

Date _____

Scripture _____

● Vision _____ ● Prophecy _____ ● Revelation _____

(Circle One)

_____
_____
_____
_____
_____
_____
_____
_____
_____
_____
_____
_____
_____
_____
_____

Date _____

Scripture _____

• Vision _____   • Prophecy _____   • Revelation _____

(Circle One)

_____
_____
_____
_____
_____
_____
_____
_____
_____
_____
_____
_____
_____
_____
_____

Date _____

Scripture _____

● Vision _____ ● Prophecy _____ ● Revelation _____

(Circle One)

_____

_____

_____

_____

_____

_____

_____

_____

_____

_____

_____

_____

_____

_____

_____

Date _____

Scripture _____

● Vision _____ ● Prophecy _____ ● Revelation _____
(Circle One)

_____

_____

_____

_____

_____

_____

_____

_____

_____

_____

_____

_____

_____

Date _____

Scripture _____

● Vision _____ ● Prophecy _____ ● Revelation _____

(Circle One)

_____

_____

_____

_____

_____

_____

_____

_____

_____

_____

_____

_____

_____

_____

_____

Date _____

Scripture _____

● Vision _____ ● Prophecy _____ ● Revelation _____
(Circle One)

_____

_____

_____

_____

_____

_____

_____

_____

_____

_____

_____

_____

_____

_____

Date _____

Scripture _____

- Vision _____ - Prophecy _____ - Revelation _____
                                                            (Circle One)

_____

_____

_____

_____

_____

_____

_____

_____

_____

_____

_____

_____

_____

_____

● Vision _____ ● Prophecy _____ ● Revelation _____
(Circle One)

_____

_____

_____

_____

_____

_____

_____

_____

_____

_____

_____

_____

_____

Date _____

Scripture _____

● Vision _____ ● Prophecy _____ ● Revelation _____

(Circle One)

_____
_____
_____
_____
_____
_____
_____
_____
_____
_____
_____
_____
_____
_____

Date _____

Scripture _____

- Vision _____ - Prophecy _____ - Revelation _____

(Circle One)

_____

_____

_____

_____

_____

_____

_____

_____

_____

_____

_____

_____

Scripture _____

● Vision _____ ● Prophecy _____ ● Revelation _____

(Circle One)

_____

_____

_____

_____

_____

_____

_____

_____

_____

_____

_____

_____

_____

_____

_____

Date

Scripture

● <u>Vision</u>   ● Prophecy   ● <u>Revelation</u>

(Circle One)

_____

_____

_____

_____

_____

_____

_____

_____

_____

_____

_____

_____

_____

_____

Date _____

Scripture _____

● Vision _____ ● Prophecy _____ ● Revelation _____
(Circle One)

_____

_____

_____

_____

_____

_____

_____

_____

_____

_____

_____

_____

_____

_____

_____

Date _____

Scripture _____

● Vision _____ ● Prophecy _____ ● Revelation _____
                                              (Circle One)

_____

_____

_____

_____

_____

_____

_____

_____

_____

_____

_____

_____

_____

Date _____

Scripture _____

● Vision _____ ● Prophecy _____ ● Revelation _____

(Circle One)

_____

_____

_____

_____

_____

_____

_____

_____

_____

_____

_____

_____

_____

_____

Date _____

Scripture _____

● Vision _____   ● Prophecy _____   ● Revelation _____
(Circle One)

_____

_____

_____

_____

_____

_____

_____

_____

_____

_____

_____

_____

_____

_____

_____

Date _____

Scripture _____

● Vision _____ ● Prophecy _____ ● Revelation _____

(Circle One)

_____

_____

_____

_____

_____

_____

_____

_____

_____

_____

_____

_____

_____

_____

_____

_____

Date _____

Scripture _____

• Vision _____ • Prophecy _____ • Revelation _____

(Circle One)

_____
_____
_____
_____
_____
_____
_____
_____
_____
_____
_____
_____
_____
_____
_____

- Vision _____
- Prophecy _____
- Revelation _____

(Circle One)

_____

_____

_____

_____

_____

_____

_____

_____

_____

_____

_____

_____

_____

Date _____

Scripture _____

● Vision _____ ● Prophecy _____ ● Revelation _____

(Circle One)

_____

_____

_____

_____

_____

_____

_____

_____

_____

_____

_____

_____

_____

Scripture _____

● Vision _____ ● Prophecy _____ ● Revelation _____

(Circle One)

_____

_____

_____

_____

_____

_____

_____

_____

_____

_____

_____

_____

_____

_____

● Vision _____ ● Prophecy _____ ● Revelation _____

(Circle One)

_____

_____

_____

_____

_____

_____

_____

_____

_____

_____

_____

_____

_____

_____

_____

_____

Date _____

Scripture _____

• Vision _____ • Prophecy _____ • Revelation _____
(Circle One)

_____

_____

_____

_____

_____

_____

_____

_____

_____

_____

_____

_____

_____

_____

_____

_____

Date _____

Scripture _____

● Vision _____   ● Prophecy _____   ● Revelation _____

(Circle One)

_____

_____

_____

_____

_____

_____

_____

_____

_____

_____

_____

_____

_____

_____

Date _____

Scripture _____

• Vision _____   • Prophecy _____   • Revelation _____

(Circle One)

_____

_____

_____

_____

_____

_____

_____

_____

_____

_____

_____

_____

_____

_____

_____

_____

Date _____

Scripture _____

● Vision _____ ● Prophecy _____ ● Revelation _____

(Circle One)

_____

_____

_____

_____

_____

_____

_____

_____

_____

_____

_____

_____

_____